D0471042

EAT SMART, LOSE WEIGHT

watch your weight the delicious way

p

This is a Parragon Publishing Book
This edition published in 2005

Parragon Publishing
Queen Street House
4 Queen Street
Bath
BA1 1HE
United Kingdom

Copyright © Parragon 2004

All rights reserved. No part of this publication may be reproduced, stored
in a retrieval system, or transmitted, in any form or by any means, electronic, mechanical,
photocopying, recording, or otherwise, without the prior permission of the copyright holder.
Created and produced by *The Bridgewater Book Company Ltd*

Parragon would like to thank Fiona Hunter.
This cookbook was written in association with Fiona Hunter, a qualified nutritionist
and dietician. Fiona has over 20 years' experience in the field of nutrition, including seven years
working for Britain's National Health Service. She now writes regularly for a number of magazines
and newspapers. Women's health issues and the problems of obesity are areas
of particular interest to Fiona.

Parragon would also like to thank Karen Thomas (photographer), Valerie Berry (home economist),
Breda Bradshaw (home economist), and Charlie Parker (marketing nutritionist).

ISBN: 1-40543-675-1

Printed in China

NOTES

V

This symbol means the recipe is suitable for vegetarians.

This book uses imperial, metric, or US cup measurements. Follow the same
units of measurement throughout; do not mix imperial and metric.

All spoon measurements are level: teaspoons are assumed to be 5 ml, and tablespoons
are assumed to be 15 ml. Unless otherwise stated, eggs and individual vegetables such as
potatoes are assumed to be medium, and pepper is freshly ground black pepper.

Recipes using raw or very lightly cooked eggs should be avoided by infants, the elderly,
pregnant women, convalescents, and anyone suffering from an illness. Pregnant and
breastfeeding women are advised to avoid eating peanuts and peanut products.

The times given are an approximate guide only. Preparation times differ according
to the techniques used by different people and the cooking times may also vary from those given.
Optional ingredients, variations, or serving suggestions have not been included in the calculations.

DISCLAIMER

Before you follow any of the advice given in this book, we recommend that you first check with your physician.
Pregnant women, women planning to become pregnant, children, diabetics, or people with other medical
conditions should always check with their physician or health care professional before embarking on any type
of diet. This book is not intended as a substitute for your physician's or dietician's advice and support, but
should complement the advice they give you. The accuracy of the nutritional information (calorie, fat, and salt)
given for each recipe is dependent on following the recipe instructions.

CONTENTS

introduction

HOW TO USE THIS COOKBOOK

Losing weight isn't always easy, but the benefits are enormous—you'll feel fitter and more confident, you'll have more energy, and you'll be healthier. The good news is that losing weight doesn't mean having to say goodbye to your favorite foods: in fact, it's important to include the foods you enjoy eating. A diet which leaves you feeling deprived, unhappy, and dissatisfied is a diet that's very quickly going to be abandoned.

With increasing pressure on our daily schedule, many of us are tempted to skip meals. Don't! You're more likely to be tempted by a snack, and at your next meal you may overeat to compensate. Remember, too, that even when time is pressing, there are many simple meals that are quick and easy to make.

On a diet, your aim should be to achieve gradual but steady and sustained weight loss. This means following a nutritionally balanced eating plan, with a target intake for women of around 1400 calories a day and for men of around 2000 calories a day.

Breakfast

Lunch

Main meal

Dessert

Following a diet can be very boring if you have to eat the same foods day after day. This book offers you a range of recipes, from breakfasts and quick lunches to entrées and even desserts. After all, you're not going to stick to a diet if you don't let yourself have a treat.

Calorie-counting can often be a case of either guesswork or complicated calculations. The recipes in this book are intended to do the hard work for you; each recipe comes with a nutritional breakdown of the calorie, total fat, and saturated fat content.

HEALTHY EATING
A BALANCED APPROACH TO HEALTHY EATING

The food we eat can have an important and lasting effect on our health. Our body needs over 40 different nutrients to stay healthy. Some, such as carbohydrates, proteins, and fats, are required in relatively large quantities, while others, such as vitamins, minerals, and trace elements, are required in minute amounts but are no less essential for health.

The best way to ensure that we get the full range of nutrients our bodies need is to eat a varied diet containing foods from each of the 5 major food groups. The secret to healthy eating and managing your weight is to get the balance right.

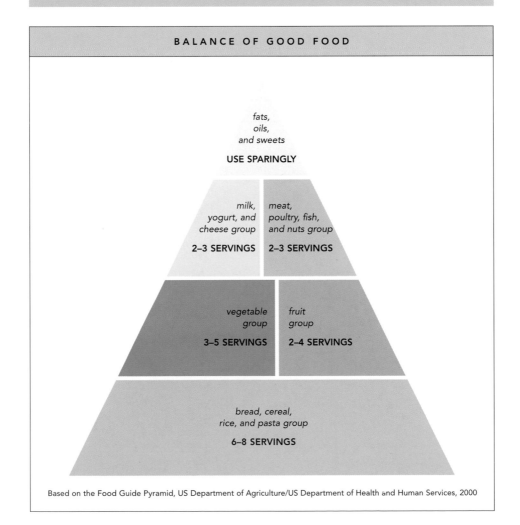

BALANCE OF GOOD FOOD

fats,
oils,
and sweets

USE SPARINGLY

milk,
yogurt, and
cheese group

2–3 SERVINGS

meat,
poultry, fish,
and nuts group

2–3 SERVINGS

vegetable
group

3–5 SERVINGS

fruit
group

2–4 SERVINGS

bread, cereal,
rice, and pasta group

6–8 SERVINGS

Based on the Food Guide Pyramid, US Department of Agriculture/US Department of Health and Human Services, 2000

7

GRAINS
(E.G. BREAD, RICE, PASTA, NOODLES, BREAKFAST CEREALS)
—KNOWN AS CARBOHYDRATES

Foods from this group should provide 45–65% of your calories each day. These foods provide carbohydrates (starch and dietary fiber), protein, vitamins, and minerals, which are all important for good health.

Choose fiber-rich complex carbohydrates such as whole grain foods—they promote proper bowel function and will help you to feel full with few calories.

Contrary to what many people believe, foods from this group are not fattening in themselves, becoming highly calorific only when eaten with lots of fat (a rich, creamy sauce with pasta, sautéed potatoes, or bread spread thickly with butter).

• Depending on your appetite and calorie requirement, aim to eat between
  6 and 8 servings from this group each day.

1 serving equals:
1 cup breakfast cereal
1 slice bread
½ cup cooked rice
½ cup cooked pasta

FRUIT AND VEGETABLES

It's no coincidence that people from Mediterranean countries, who eat almost twice the amount of fruit and vegetables we do, live longer and remain healthier. Fruit and vegetables provide vitamins and minerals, dietary fiber, and other important substances.

The Food Guide Pyramid recommends that we should all aim to eat 2–4 servings of fruit and 3–5 servings of vegetables a day. This has been proved to help prevent a number of diseases, including heart disease and several forms of cancer.

Apart from being excellent providers of vitamins and minerals, most fruit and vegetables are fat-free and wonderfully low in calories. Make the most of them and look out for new recipes and ideas for cooking them—try poaching, baking, or broiling fruits as an alternative to eating them raw.

- Aim to eat at least 2 servings of fruit and 3 servings of vegetables a day.
- Adopt a rainbow approach—different colored fruit and vegetables provide different vitamins and minerals.
- Frozen, canned, and dried fruits and vegetables, as well as juices, are all useful in helping you reach your daily target.

1 serving equals:

FRUIT		VEGETABLES	
1 medium apple, banana, orange, or pear	½ cup chopped, cooked, or canned fruit ¾ cup fruit juice	1 cup raw leafy vegetables	½ cup other vegetables (cooked or raw) ¾ cup vegetable juice

MILK AND DAIRY
(E.G. MILK, YOGURT, CHEESE)

Dairy products are an important source of calcium, essential for strong bones and teeth. Many people, especially teenage girls, fail to eat enough calcium to meet their recommended daily requirement—putting them at risk of the bone disease osteoporosis in later life.

Dairy foods also provide protein, vitamin A, phosphorus, vitamin D, and vitamin B_2. Foods in this group can be high in fat, particularly saturated fat—choose reduced-fat and lowfat alternatives such as skim and lowfat milk. Calcium is contained in the non-creamy portion of milk, so the calcium remains when the fat is removed to make reduced-fat products—in fact, pint for pint skim milk contains slightly more calcium than whole milk. Remember that this group does not include butter, eggs, and cream.

• Aim to eat 2–3 servings from this group a day.
• Choose lowfat and reduced-fat varieties whenever possible.

1 serving equals:
1 cup milk
1 cup yogurt
1½ oz natural cheese, such as Cheddar
2 oz processed cheese, such as American

MEAT AND BEANS
(E.G. MEAT, POULTRY, FISH,
EGGS, DRY BEANS, AND NUTS)

Foods from this group provide protein, needed for the production of enzymes, antibodies, and hormones. In short, protein is the building block of the body. Foods in this group are also a good source of iron, needed by the blood to circulate oxygen around the body. Low iron stores in the body can cause tiredness, lethargy, and possibly anemia.

- Aim to eat 2–3 servings from this group a day.
- Meat should be lean with any visible fat removed before cooking, and the skin should be removed from poultry.
- Meat can be fresh, frozen, or part of a prepared meal, but limit your intake of high-fat processed meats, such as bacon and sausages.
- Aim to eat 1–2 servings of oil-rich fish, such as salmon or tuna, a week. They are rich in omega-3 fatty acids, and help to reduce the risk of heart disease.
- Vegetarians should eat a variety of different protein foods to ensure they get all the nutrients they need.

1 serving equals approximately:
2–3 oz cooked lean meat, poultry, or fish*

*1 oz of lean meat, poultry or fish is equal to:
½ cup of cooked dry beans, ½ cup of tofu, 1 egg,
2 tbsp of peanut butter, or ⅓ cup of nuts

11

FOODS CONTAINING FATS AND SUGARS

Small amounts of fat are vital in our diet to provide essential fatty acids and to facilitate the absorption of fat-soluble vitamins, but a high-fat diet is known to increase the risk of heart disease, certain types of cancer, and obesity. A diet that is rich in saturated fats, found in foods such as fatty cuts of meat and meat products, full-fat dairy products, and butter and some types of margarine increases the levels of cholesterol in the blood.

Weight for weight, fat provides twice as many calories as carbohydrate or protein. There is also some evidence to suggest that calories eaten as fat are more likely to be laid down as body fat than calories from protein or carbohydrate. The good news is that these days low in fat doesn't have to mean low in taste. There are easy ways to trim the fat from your diet (see page 20) without giving up the foods you enjoy.

Sugar provides "empty" calories—calories that provide nothing else in the way of protein, fiber, vitamins, or minerals, and calories that most of us could do without. So it makes sense to cut down on it where you can. Sugar and sugary foods also increase the risk of tooth decay, especially when eaten between meals.

- Total fat should provide less than 30% of your total calories each day. For a woman eating 2000 calories a day, this amounts to about 65 g of fat or less.
- Saturated fat should provide less than 10% of your total fat intake. For a woman eating 2000 calories a day, this amounts to about 20 g of fat or less.
- Look at the nutritional labeling on food packaging to check the fat content of the food. Try to choose foods that are low in saturated fat.
- Avoid adding sugar to food.

DIETARY FIBER

Although it passes through our digestive tract unchanged, fiber is essential for a healthy digestive system.

Fiber can be divided into 2 groups: insoluble fiber and soluble fiber. Insoluble fiber is found mainly in wheat, whole-grain cereals, fruit and vegetables, and dried beans, peas, and lentils. It has the effect of holding or absorbing water, which helps to prevent constipation and diverticular disease. It also speeds up the rate at which waste material is passed through the body, and this is believed to play an important role in preventing colon cancer by reducing the length of time that cancer-causing toxins stay within the digestive system.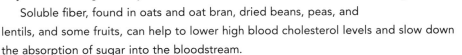

Soluble fiber, found in oats and oat bran, dried beans, peas, and lentils, and some fruits, can help to lower high blood cholesterol levels and slow down the absorption of sugar into the bloodstream.

The recommended daily intake of dietary fiber for men and women is 25–35 g.

EASY WAYS TO INCREASE YOUR FIBER INTAKE:

• Choose a whole grain cereal such as oatmeal, granola, or bran flakes for breakfast. Pick one that provides 3 g of fiber or more per serving.

• Choose whole wheat, whole oat, or whole rye bread. Bread may be brown, but this doesn't necessarily mean that it is high in fiber—look for the words "whole grain" or "whole wheat" on the label.

• Eat more dried beans, peas, and lentils such as red kidney beans and chickpeas.

• Eat a minimum of 2 servings of fruit and 3 servings of vegetables a day.

• Eat dried fruit as snack between meals or add it to your breakfast cereal.

• Use brown rather than white rice, and whole wheat pasta.

SALT (SODIUM CHLORIDE)

Sodium plays a vital role in the body's fluid balance as well as being involved in muscle and nerve activity. Almost all of us, however, consume far more than is good for us. A high salt intake is believed to be a major factor in the development of high blood pressure, which increases the risk of stroke and heart disease.

- Experts recommend moderating your daily salt intake to no more than 2400 mg. This is only 1 teaspoon of salt, which is around half our current average intake. Healthy adults actually only need less than ¼ teaspoon of salt daily to meet their sodium requirement.
- Around 80% of the sodium in our diet comes from processed foods—1 small can of chicken soup, for instance, can contain over half the recommended daily amount.
- Train your taste buds to enjoy foods with less salt. Try using herbs and spices to enhance the flavor of food.
- As a general rule, foods that contain more than 500 mg sodium per serving are high in sodium. Foods that contain less than 100 mg sodium per serving are low in sodium. Always read the nutritional labeling on packaging.

WATER

Water is vital to good health. Unlike some other nutrients, the human body does not store water, so you need to drink a regular supply.

Some foods, particularly fruit and vegetables, contain quite a lot of water—a slice of watermelon, for instance, is 92% water and an apple 84%—and eating them can

help replace some of the water lost by the body. We still need to drink around 8–10 glasses of fluid each day to prevent the body from becoming dehydrated.

Around 85% of our brain tissue is water—which explains why even mild dehydration can lead to problems such as headaches, lethargy, dizziness, and an inability to concentrate. Long-term dehydration can lead to digestive problems, kidney problems, and joint pain. Relying on thirst to tell you when you need to take a drink is not always a good idea—by the time you feel thirsty, your body is probably already mildly dehydrated.

- Drink at least 8–10 glasses (a glass is about 8 fl oz/225 ml) of fluid a day.
- Don't always rely on thirst as a sign that you need to take a drink.
- Eating plenty of fruit and vegetables will help increase your fluid intake.
- Take water breaks rather than coffee breaks at regular intervals during the day.
- Keeping a bottle of water on your desk at work will remind you to take a drink.
- To check to see you are drinking enough fluid, look at your urine—if you're drinking enough, it should be a light yellow color. Dark yellow urine is a sign you're not drinking enough.
- Drink plenty of water before, during, and after taking exercise—especially in warm weather.

ALCOHOL

Alcohol is not forbidden on a diet, but it is worth remembering that for most of us willpower dissolves in alcohol! A glass of wine may be only 100 calories, but the trouble is that 1 glass easily leads to another, and after a couple of drinks it's easy to forget about your good intentions to eat healthily. If you drink alcohol, do so in moderation, which means no more than 1 serving per day for women and no more than 2 servings per day for men.

1 serving equals:
5 fl oz wine
12 fl oz regular beer
1½ fl oz spirits

8 STEPS TO A HEALTHY DIET

Enjoy your food

Eat a variety of different foods

Eat the right amount to achieve a healthy weight

Eat plenty of complex carbohydrates and fiber

Eat plenty of fruit and vegetables

Don't eat too many foods that contain a lot of fat

Don't have sugary foods and drinks too often

Drink alcohol in moderation

LOSING WEIGHT SAFELY

If you're trying to lose weight, you're not alone. In 1999, statistics showed that 61% of adults in the US were classified as overweight (BMI over 25—see page 17) or obese (BMI over 30). The number of obese people in the US has doubled in the last 2 decades. Many nutritionists believe that the reason for this alarming rise is due not to our eating more, but to our doing less. Modern technology and labor-saving devices mean that we're much less active than we used to be.

Our weight is a reflection of the balance between the energy (calories) we consume and the energy we use. Our energy intake is determined by the amount and type of food we eat. Our energy expenditure is determined by a combination of our resting metabolic rate and the amount of calories we burn in day-to-day activities.

The resting metabolic rate is the amount of energy our body needs during rest or sleep. This is similar to the fuel used by a car when the engine is idling but the car is stationary.

If our energy intake equals our energy expenditure, our body weight will remain the same, but if our intake exceeds our expenditure, the excess energy is stored in the body as fat (see below).

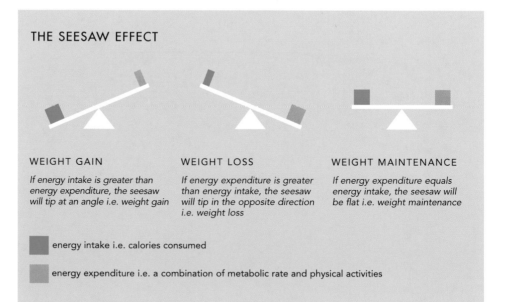

THE SEESAW EFFECT

WEIGHT GAIN

If energy intake is greater than energy expenditure, the seesaw will tip at an angle i.e. weight gain

WEIGHT LOSS

If energy expenditure is greater than energy intake, the seesaw will tip in the opposite direction i.e. weight loss

WEIGHT MAINTENANCE

If energy expenditure equals energy intake, the seesaw will be flat i.e. weight maintenance

energy intake i.e. calories consumed

energy expenditure i.e. a combination of metabolic rate and physical activities

THE IDEAL RATE OF WEIGHT LOSS

Experts agree the best and safest way to lose weight is slowly and steadily—between 1–2 lb (0.5–1 kg) a week is the ideal rate. If you lose too much weight too quickly, there is a danger of losing lean muscle tissue as well as fat. Since our basal metabolic rate (the number of calories the body needs to function) is related to the amount of lean muscle tissue we have, it's a good idea to do whatever we can to preserve it.

HOW LOW SHOULD YOU GO?

The total number of calories we need to eat each day varies, depending on a number of factors, including age, weight, sex, activity levels, body composition, and metabolic rate. As a general guide, women need around 2000 calories a day and men need 2500. To lose 1 lb (0.5 kg) a week, you need to reduce your calorie intake by 500 calories a day. Diets that restrict calories too severely (fewer than 1200 calories a day) are not recommended.

HOW YOU SHAPE UP

Although most of us can get a pretty good idea of whether we need to lose weight or not just by looking in the mirror, you can get a more accurate assessment by calculating your Body Mass Index or waist circumference (see panel below).

HOW YOU SHAPE UP

BMI (Body Mass Index) =

$$\frac{\text{weight in pounds}}{\text{(height in inches)} \times \text{(height in inches)}} \times 703$$

For example, a person who weighs 145 pounds and is 5 feet 8 inches tall has a BMI of 22.

$$\frac{145 \text{ pounds}}{\text{(68 inches)} \times \text{(68 inches)}} \times 703 = 22$$

Below 18.5	*underweight*
18.5–24.9	*normal weight range*
25.0–29.9	*overweight*
Over 30	*obese*

(Source: Centers for Disease Control and Prevention, 2003)

WAIST CIRCUMFERENCE

Men	**Women**
Waist circumference over 37 in (94 cm) *indicates a slight health risk*	Waist circumference over 31½ in (80 cm) *indicates a slight health risk*
Waist circumference over 40 in (102 cm) *indicates a substantial health risk*	Waist circumference over 34½ in (88 cm) *indicates a substantial health risk*

THE 3 MAIN REASONS THAT DIETS FAIL
Setting unrealistic goals—if you set unrealistic goals, you're more likely to become disheartened and give up. Aim for a slow but steady weight loss of 1–2 lb (0.5–1 kg) a week. If you lose too much weight too quickly, there's a danger of losing lean muscle tissue as well as fat.
Following the wrong sort of diet—however tempting they may seem, crash diets just don't work. Although you may lose weight initially, you'll find you will end up putting on not just the weight you originally lost but more.
Not eating enough—a mistake people often make is to reduce their calorie intake too severely. Overly strict diets are difficult to stick to in the long run, they're not necessary, and they're not healthy. If you restrict your calories too severely, the chances are that you'll end up missing out on important nutrients.

UNDERSTANDING YOUR RELATIONSHIP WITH FOOD

Often we eat out of habit or to satisfy emotional needs rather than because we are hungry. We use food to celebrate, to relieve boredom, or to make us feel better when we're unhappy or lonely. Certain people, places, moods, and situations can also prompt us to eat.

Keeping a food diary will help you to identify these external cues. Buy a notebook and divide the pages into columns as shown below. Keep a record of everything you eat and drink and how you feel for 2 weeks.

FOOD DIARY					
Date and time	Where you are	What you are doing and who you're with	How you feel (e.g. tired, unhappy, bored)	What you ate	How hungry are you? On a scale of 1–5: 1=hungry 5=not hungry
Wednesday 3.30pm	At home	Nothing	Bored	Package of potato chips	5
Thursday 10.30am	At work	Trying to meet tight deadline	Stressed	Chocolate bar	4

At the end of 2 weeks, review your diary and make a list of all the triggers that prompt you to eat when you're not really hungry.

Once you have identified these trigger factors, you can start to think about solutions and ways to avoid those situations in future. Work out strategies that will help avoid or change the way you behave when faced with these triggers. If, for instance, you find you get home after work so hungry that you end up eating a family-size package of cheesy snacks while preparing the evening meal, plan ahead. Have a healthy snack such as a banana or yogurt before you leave the office so you won't feel so hungry when you get home. If your diary reveals that you use food as a way of making yourself feel better when you're unhappy or depressed, make a list of non-food related activities that will help lift your spirits when you're feeling low. Rent a video, have a manicure, or take a long leisurely bath rather than reaching for a chocolate bar.

GETTING FITTER

A combination of diet and exercise is by far the best way to lose weight. Exercise burns calories and it also helps develop muscle tissue. Muscle is metabolically more active than your body's fat stores (it uses more calories than fat). In other words, the more muscle you have, the more calories your body burns. Exercise will also help to improve your body shape and tone and help you maintain your weight loss.

If you haven't done any exercise before, take it easy when you first start. If you begin with something that is beyond your levels of fitness, you're more likely to become discouraged and give up.

Exercise doesn't necessarily mean getting hot and sweaty in the gym. Making small changes to your normal routine—such as walking instead of driving, or taking the stairs rather than the elevator—can make a big difference. Walking briskly for 20 to 30 minutes a day, 5 days a week, will burn the equivalent of 12 lb (5.4 kg) of fat in a year. Setting yourself the goal of taking 10,000 steps a day can be a good way to start.

Choose something you enjoy and that fits in with your lifestyle—you're more likely to stick with it. And try to persuade a friend or family member to exercise with you. If you make a commitment to a friend, you're less likely to back out.

The scales never lie, but they can distort the truth because muscle tissue weighs more than fat. If you're doing a lot of exercise and building muscle tissue, the scales may not move—don't be disheartened. You'll notice your body becoming more toned and shapely, your clothes will begin to fit differently as you lose inches, and—most importantly—you will be healthier.

TRIMMING THE FAT

Fat provides twice as many calories as either protein or carbohydrate, which is why the most effective way of reducing calories is to limit the amount of fat you use.

- Start with lowfat ingredients—white fish, shellfish, chicken, and lean meat are all good choices.
- Trim off visible fat from meat before cooking and remove the skin from poultry. Avoid red meat that has too much fat or marbling.
- Choose lowfat cooking techniques—poach, braise, steam, broil, or stir-fry. Marinades are a good way of adding extra flavor without fat.
- Invest in a good heavy-bottom nonstick pan and remember that oil expands once it gets hot—so when you're softening onions or vegetables you don't need to add as much as you might think. Use a vegetable or olive oil nonstick cooking spray for dishes that require light sautéing.
- You don't need fat to add flavor—use plenty of fresh herbs and spices in your cooking. Adding a squeeze of fresh lemon juice just before serving can give food a real flavor boost.
- Bulk out savory dishes by adding plenty of vegetables. They are low in calories and provide essential vitamins.
- Use reduced- and lowfat alternatives such as reduced-fat cheese, skim milk, and lowfat yogurts where available.
- To make gravies and sauces creamy, add yogurt or ricotta rather than cream. Stir in at the end of cooking to prevent curdling.
- Using cheese with a strong flavor, such as sharp Cheddar, Parmesan, or blue cheese, will mean that you need to add less.
- Don't be afraid to use high-fat foods such as cheese and bacon: you will need only small quantities to add a lot of flavor.
- 1 tablespoon of French dressing contains 97 calories and about 11 g of fat. Use sparingly or choose a lowfat dressing.

ESSENTIAL TIPS FOR LOSING WEIGHT FOREVER

1 / **Recognize why you overeat**—before you reach for a chocolate bar or slice of cake, ask yourself if you're really hungry. Keep a food diary (see page 18) to help you identify danger times when you are more likely to overeat.

2 / **Believe you can do it**—a recent study found that people who believed they could lose weight and keep it off were more likely to succeed. Try to visualize the new, slimmer you and keep that image in your mind.

3 / **Eat slowly and chew your food thoroughly**—the brain takes 15 minutes to get the message that your stomach has had enough to eat. If you eat too quickly, your stomach fills up before your brain knows you are full, and you end up eating too much.

4 / **Never skip meals** or let yourself get overhungry. If you do, you'll be more tempted to snack and overeat at your next meal. Aim to eat 3 small to medium-size meals a day plus 2 or 3 small, healthy snacks.

5 / **Always eat breakfast**—if you skip breakfast, you're more likely to snack during the morning and overeat at lunch.

6 / **Get fruity**—fruit and vegetables are a dieter's best friend: they're low in calories and fat-free. Aim to eat at least 5 servings a day. Be adventurous and try something new. Look for recipes and ideas for new ways of cooking fruit or vegetables.

7 / **Stack up with starches and fill up with fiber**—choose fiber-rich varieties such as whole-wheat bread and whole-grain cereals whenever possible. These provide slow-release energy, which helps keep blood sugar levels stable.

8 / **Be prepared**—make sure your cupboards and freezer are full of healthy foods and have plenty of low-calorie snacks available.

9 / **Don't feel that 1 bad day will ruin the whole diet**—life is full of ups and downs, so if you do lapse on the odd bad day, be a little stricter with yourself the following day.

10 / **Never go shopping on an empty stomach**—always write a list and stick to it! Don't buy foods you know you won't be able to resist.

11 / **Don't deny yourself the foods you enjoy**—just eat them in moderation.

12 / **Drink at least 8 glasses of water a day**—it's easy to confuse thirst with hunger. When you think you're feeling hungry, try drinking a large glass of water first.

13 / **Trim the fat**—fat is a dieter's biggest enemy. Whenever possible, choose products that are low in fat.

14 / **Make use of every opportunity you can to stay active**—use the stairs instead of the elevator or escalator, get off the bus 1 stop early and walk the rest of the way home. Small changes all add up and can make a big difference.

Breakfasts

Many nutritionists consider breakfast to be the most important meal of the day, particularly for anyone watching their weight. Cutting calories by skipping breakfast is a false economy—if you miss breakfast, you're much more likely to get hungry midmorning and overeat at lunchtime. Studies show that people who eat breakfast in the morning are less likely to be overweight than those who skip it. Miss breakfast and you're also missing out on the opportunity to boost your intake of several important vitamins and minerals. People who regularly eat breakfast have been shown to have a higher intake of vitamins B_1, B_2, niacin, B_6, folic acid, B_{12}, C, and D, as well as the minerals iron and calcium, when compared with those who eat nothing. Other studies show that people who eat breakfast are less likely to suffer from colds and flu.

Dried fruit compote

prep 5 minutes + 3 hours soaking | **serves** 1

Opposite
foreground: Dried
fruit compote;
background:
Apple and
blueberry granola

⅓ cup dried fruit (apricots, figs,
    prunes), coarsely chopped
2 cardamom pods, lightly crushed
scant ½ cup boiling water
juice 2 oranges, about ½ cup
1 tbsp fat-free plain yogurt

1. Place the fruit and crushed cardamom in
a large heatproof bowl. Pour over the water
and orange juice and let soak for at least
3 hours.
2. Remove the cardamom and serve with
the yogurt swirled in.

COOK'S TIP
• *Any type of dried fruit combination can*
be used to make the compote.

Apple and blueberry granola

prep 5 minutes + overnight soaking | **serves** 1

scant ¼ cup lowfat granola
generous ⅓ cup apple juice
1 apple, cored
½ cup blueberries or blackberries
3 tbsp lowfat plain yogurt

1. Place the granola in a bowl and pour
over the apple juice, then cover and put in
the refrigerator to chill overnight.
2. Coarsely grate the apple and add to
the granola. Stir in the berries and lowfat
yogurt and serve.

NUTRITION INFORMATION
per serving

calories	fat	sat fat
130	0.3 g	trace

NUTRITION INFORMATION
per serving

calories	fat	sat fat
252	2.6 g	0.8 g

Creamy mushrooms on toast

prep 5 minutes | **cook** 10 minutes | **serves** 1

½ tsp olive oil
1–3 scallions, trimmed and finely chopped (optional)
1 small garlic clove, peeled and finely chopped or crushed (optional)
3½ oz (100 g) whole white mushrooms (or other mushrooms, cut into fourths)
1 strip lean bacon
1 tbsp chopped fresh parsley
freshly ground black pepper, to taste
1 slice whole wheat or whole grain bread, toasted

1. Add the oil to a small, lidded, nonstick pan over low heat.
2. Add the scallion, garlic, if using, and mushrooms and stir until blended. Put a lid on the pan and continue cooking, shaking the pan to mix the ingredients. If necessary, add 1 tablespoon of water.
3. Cook the mixture for 5–10 minutes or until the mushrooms have changed color and released their juices.
4. Pan-fry the bacon quickly in a nonstick skillet and add to the mushrooms.
5. Stir in the parsley and pepper and serve on hot toast, topped with the bacon.

COOK'S TIPS
• *Add flavor by using portobello mushrooms in this recipe. Just trim off the gills before cooking to prevent discoloration.*
• *To dress this dish up for dinner, you can substitute white wine for the water added during cooking, or add a little light sour cream (1 tsp adds an extra 6–7 calories and around 0.4 g of fat to the total for the dish).*

NUTRITION INFORMATION

per serving

calories	fat	sat fat
150	6.7 g	1.6 g

Ginger fruit teabread with mashed banana

(V) | **prep** 10 minutes + 2 hours soaking + 2 hours cooling | **cook** 1 hour 15 minutes | **prep ahead** 24 hours | **serves** 5 (*10 slices*)

⅓ cup no-soak dried apricots, coarsely chopped
scant ⅓ cup no-soak jumbo golden raisins
¼ cup pitted no-soak prunes, coarsely chopped
1¼ cups strongly brewed tea without milk, left to cool
1½ cups all-purpose flour
2 tsp baking powder
1 tsp ground ginger
generous ½ cup raw brown sugar
1 medium egg, beaten

for the topping (per serving)
1 small banana, mashed

1. Preheat the oven to 350°F/180°C. Lightly grease a 2-lb (900-g) loaf pan and line the
bottom with parchment paper.
2. Put the dried fruits in a large measuring cup or bowl, then pour over the tea and let
stand for at least 2 hours, stirring occasionally.
3. Put the flour, baking powder, ginger, sugar, and egg into a food processor and blend for
a couple of minutes, or until well mixed. Add the dried fruits and blend again until mixed.
4. Turn the mixture into the prepared pan, then level the surface and brush lightly with
water. Place on the center shelf of the oven for 1¼ hours, or until cooked.
5. Let the cake cool in the pan for 10–15 minutes. Loosen the edges with a knife and then
turn out onto a wire rack to cool.
6. When cool, cut off slices and serve topped with mashed banana.

COOK'S TIP
• *Any dried fruit can be used as an alternative to the apricots and golden raisins.*

NUTRITION INFORMATION

per serving

(⅒ *of loaf (2 slices), topped with banana*)

calories	fat	sat fat
240	1.3 g	0.3 g

Soups, salads, and light lunches

However busy you are, it's important to make the time to sit down and enjoy a proper lunch. Tempting as it is to skip meals when you're busy, you're more likely to end up snacking on chocolate or cookies later in the afternoon if you do. Try to include at least 1 serving of vegetables and 1 serving of fruit at lunchtime. Drinking a large glass of still or sparkling water before you start eating will help fill your stomach and reduce the risk of overeating.

Carrot and cumin soup

(V) | **prep** 5 minutes | **cook** 30 minutes | **serves** 1 *(or 2 small appetizers)*

1 medium–large carrot, peeled and finely chopped
1 small garlic clove, peeled and chopped
1 medium–large shallot, peeled and finely chopped
1 ripe tomato, skinned (see COOK'S TIP) and chopped
½ tsp ground cumin
generous ¾ cup vegetable stock
1 bouquet garni (see COOK'S TIP)
freshly ground black pepper, to taste
2 tsp dry sherry (optional)
1 tbsp light sour cream, to serve (optional)
pinch of cumin, to garnish

1. Put all the ingredients except the sherry and sour cream in a lidded pan.
2. Bring to simmering point over high heat, then reduce the heat, put the lid on, and simmer for 30 minutes, or until the vegetables are tender. Cool slightly and remove the bouquet garni.
3. Pour the soup into an electric blender and purée until smooth.
4. Return to the pan, then add the sherry, if using, and reheat. Taste for seasoning. Serve with a swirl of sour cream, if using, and a pinch of cumin.

COOK'S TIPS
• *To skin a tomato, make a cross with a knife across the stem end and pop into boiling water for a few minutes. Drain, place the tomato in an ice bath, and then slip the skin off.*
• *To make a bouquet garni, tie a bay leaf and a few sprigs of fresh parsley and thyme in a bunch or in a piece of cheesecloth.*

PREPARE AHEAD
• *Complete to the end of step 3, then cool. Cover and refrigerate for up to 24 hours. Continue with step 4.*

NUTRITION INFORMATION

per serving

(including the sherry and sour cream)

calories	fat	sat fat
135	4.2 g	0.4 g

Spiced lentil and vegetable soup

(V) | **prep** 5 minutes | **cook** 50 minutes–1 hour | **serves** 1

1 tsp vegetable or olive oil
1 tsp mild curry paste
1½ cups vegetable stock
1 medium onion, peeled and chopped
scant ¼ cup dried split red lentils
1 medium carrot, peeled and chopped
1 small parsnip or potato, peeled and chopped
1 medium celery stalk, chopped
1 tsp tomato paste

1. Heat the oil in a lidded, nonstick pan, then add the curry paste and garlic and stir over low heat for 1 minute.
2. Add the stock and stir to combine, then add the rest of the ingredients and bring to a simmer over medium-high heat.
3. Reduce the heat, then put the lid on and cook for 40–50 minutes, or until the lentils are tender.
4. Remove half or all the soup from the pan (according to taste—see COOK'S TIP) and purée in an electric blender. Return the soup to the pan and reheat gently to serve.

COOK'S TIP
• *By blending only half the quantity, you get a nice thick soup, which is still chunky.*

NUTRITION INFORMATION

per serving

calories	fat	sat fat
280	6.8 g	0.1 g

Roast mushroom and garlic soup
with whole wheat croutons

Ⓥ | **prep** 2 minutes | **cook** 30–40 minutes | **serves** 1

2 large open-cap mushrooms, wiped clean
2 garlic cloves, peeled
1 slice whole wheat bread, cut into small cubes
1 tsp olive oil
¼ oz (10 g) dried porcini mushrooms
1 cup vegetable stock
1 tsp fresh thyme leaves
1 tsp vegetarian Worcestershire sauce
freshly ground black pepper, to taste
1 tsp light sour cream (optional)
few sprigs of fresh thyme, to garnish

1. Preheat the oven to 350°F/180°C.
2. Loosely wrap the open-cap mushrooms and garlic in foil and place in the oven. Bake for 10 minutes, then open the foil and bake for an additional 5 minutes.
3. To prepare the croutons, drizzle the bread cubes with the oil, then place on a baking sheet and bake for 10–15 minutes, or until golden brown.
4. Meanwhile, put the porcini mushrooms, stock, and thyme leaves in a lidded pan.
5. When the open-cap mushrooms are cooked, remove from the oven, then slice and add them to the pan with the Worcestershire sauce, roasted garlic, the mushroom juices, and pepper to taste.
6. Cover and simmer for 15 minutes over low heat.
7. Let cool slightly and purée half the soup in an electric blender for a few seconds. Return to the pan and reheat gently. Stir in the sour cream, if using, and adjust the pepper to taste.
8. Transfer to a bowl, sprinkle over the croutons and sprigs of thyme, and serve.

COOK'S TIP
• *If you can get them, try using portobello mushrooms for this recipe to maximize the flavor.*

NUTRITION INFORMATION

per serving

calories	fat	sat fat
140	5.4 g	1.2 g

Spiced chicken and apricot salad

prep 10 minutes | **cook** 10 minutes | **serves** 1

scant ¼ cup, dry weight, brown basmati rice
1 tbsp lowfat plain yogurt
2 tsp mango chutney
1 tsp mild curry paste
2¾ oz (75 g) cooked skinless chicken breast, diced
2 scallions, trimmed and shredded
½ celery stalk, finely chopped
scant ¼ cup no-soak dried apricots, coarsely chopped
1 oz (25 g) fresh baby spinach leaves

1. Rinse the rice in cold water and put in a small pan. Cover with water and bring to a boil, then reduce the heat and simmer, covered, for 10 minutes, or until just tender. Drain well, then turn the rice into a bowl.
2. Mix the yogurt, mango chutney, and curry paste together.
3. Add the chicken, scallions, celery, apricots, and yogurt mixture to the cooked rice. Stir the mixture well.
4. Serve warm on a bed of baby spinach.

COOK'S TIP
• *Brown rice adds more fiber and B vitamins, but if you prefer you can use white rice. Different types of rice will have different cooking times, so follow the directions on the package.*

NUTRITION INFORMATION

per serving

calories	fat	sat fat
290	6.4 g	1.3 g

Lentil and goat cheese salad

(V) | **prep** 10 minutes | **cook** 20–30 minutes | **serves** 1

scant ¼ cup dried Puy lentils
1 bay leaf
2 scallions, trimmed and finely chopped
1¾ oz (50 g) red bell pepper, diced
1 tbsp chopped fresh parsley
3½ oz (100 g) cherry tomatoes, sliced in half
1¾ oz (50 g) arugula
1¼ oz (35 g) goat cheese, sliced or crumbled

for the dressing
1 tsp olive oil
1 tsp balsamic vinegar
½ tsp runny honey
1 garlic clove, peeled and crushed or finely chopped

1. Rinse the lentils and put in a medium-size pan. Add the bay leaf and cover with plenty of cold water. Bring to a boil, then reduce the heat and simmer for 20–30 minutes, or until the lentils are tender.
2. Drain the lentils and transfer to a bowl. Add the scallions, bell pepper, parsley, and cherry tomatoes. Mix well.
3. Whisk together the oil, vinegar, honey, and garlic and stir into the lentils. Serve on a bed of arugula, with the goat cheese sprinkled over.

COOK'S TIP
• *If time is short, replace the dried lentils with 2¾ oz (75 g), drained weight, canned cooked lentils.*

NUTRITION INFORMATION

per serving

calories	fat	sat fat
220	9.3 g	3.8 g

Tunisian poached egg

(V) | **prep** 5 minutes | **cook** 20 minutes | **serves** 1

1 tsp olive oil
1 small green bell pepper, seeded and thinly sliced
1 small red or yellow bell pepper, seeded and thinly sliced
1 small onion or large shallot, peeled and thinly sliced
7 oz (200 g) canned tomatoes, chopped
1 tsp ground cumin
freshly ground black pepper, to taste
1 small egg
pinch of sweet paprika (optional)
2 mini pita breads or 1 slice whole-wheat bread, toasted

1. Heat the oil in a nonstick skillet and sauté the bell peppers and onion over medium-high heat for about 5 minutes, stirring occasionally, or until they are soft and turning golden.
2. Add the tomatoes, cumin, and pepper to taste and stir to combine, then cook for an additional 5 minutes.
3. Meanwhile, heat water in a skillet to a depth of 1¼ inches (3 cm) to simmering point, and break the egg into the pan. Keep the water barely simmering and poach the egg for 3 minutes, or until the white is cooked.
4. Serve the bell peppers in an individual gratin dish with the egg on top, sprinkle with the paprika, if using, and season to taste with pepper. Serve with warmed pita bread or toast.

COOK'S TIPS
• *Make sure the egg is very fresh, or it will not poach well.*
• *If you have time, or if you are already using the oven, you can transfer the bell peppers to an ovenproof gratin dish at the end of step 1 and break the egg into a well in the middle of them. Then cook at 375°F/190°C for 10 minutes, or until the egg is cooked but still soft.*

NUTRITION INFORMATION

per serving

calories	fat	sat fat
290	10 g	2.3 g

Thai fish cakes with sweet chili dipping sauce

prep 5 minutes + 30 minutes chilling | **cook** 6 minutes | **serves** 1 (*makes 2 cakes*)

for the fish cakes
3½ oz (100 g) skinless cod or haddock fillet
1 scallion, trimmed and finely chopped
¼ fresh red chili, seeded and finely chopped
¼ tsp finely chopped fresh gingerroot
1 small garlic clove, peeled and crushed or finely chopped
2 tsp lime juice
1 tbsp chopped fresh cilantro leaves
1 tsp vegetable oil

for the salad garnish
½ small carrot, peeled and finely sliced into strips
2 scallions, trimmed and finely sliced into strips
1¼ inches (3 cm) cucumber, finely sliced into strips
lime wedges, to garnish

for the chili sauce
½ tsp finely chopped fresh gingerroot
½ fresh mild red chili, seeded and finely chopped
2 tsp brown sugar
½ tsp light soy sauce
1 tbsp dry sherry

1. Put all the fish cake ingredients except the oil in a food processor and blend until smooth.
2. With wet hands, divide the mixture in half and shape into 2 fish cakes. Put on a plate, then cover and chill for at least 30 minutes.
3. Prepare the salad garnish.
4. Put all the sauce ingredients in a food processor and blend until smooth (or shake them up in a lidded jar).
5. Heat the oil in a shallow, nonstick skillet and cook the fish cakes over medium heat for about 3 minutes. Turn and cook for an additional 3 minutes, or until firm. Serve garnished with salad and lime wedges, and with the sauce on the side.

COOK'S TIP
• *Make sure the fish cake mixture is well blended to ensure the fish cakes hold their shape while cooking.*

NUTRITION INFORMATION
per serving (i.e. 2 cakes)

calories	fat	sat fat
200	4 g	0.6 g

Meat and
fish entrées

Healthy eating doesn't have to mean spending hours in the kitchen. With a little thought and forward planning, there are plenty of simple dishes that you can assemble and cook in a matter of minutes. However, if you do have the time available, preparing a meal in the evening can be a relaxing and creative end to the day. Variety may be the spice of life, but it's also the key to a healthy, well-balanced diet, so don't fall into the trap of eating the same meals week in, week out. If time is at a premium, it helps to be organized. Make sure your cupboards and freezer are well stocked and plan ahead: try to write a menu for the week at the weekend when you have a little more time. Remember, vegetables are a dieter's best friend, so supplement your entrée with plenty of vegetables or salad.

Chicken and pine nuts with saffron couscous and lemon dressing

prep 10 minutes | **cook** 10 minutes, including soaking time | **serves** 1

1–2 saffron strands
1¾ oz (50 g), dry weight, couscous
2 tsp golden raisins
½ cup boiling hot chicken or vegetable stock

for the dressing
1 tsp finely chopped fresh cilantro leaves
juice of ½ lemon
1 tsp olive oil

1 x 3½ oz (100 g) chicken breast fillet, cut into 8 strips
¼ cup corn kernels
1 tsp pine nuts
10 cherry tomatoes, cut into fourths
2 scallions, trimmed and chopped
fresh cilantro leaves, to garnish

1. Put the saffron, couscous, and golden raisins in a heatproof bowl and pour over the hot stock. Stir once and let stand for 15 minutes.
2. Meanwhile, whisk together the dressing ingredients.
3. Brown the chicken strips on all sides in a preheated nonstick skillet over high heat for about 4 minutes.
4. Reduce the heat to medium, add the corn and pine nuts and cook for an additional 2 minutes, stirring once or twice. Remove the chicken from the skillet and set aside.
5. Fluff up the couscous with a fork and add to the skillet with the tomatoes, dressing, and scallions. Heat for 1 minute, or until warmed through, stirring gently.
6. Spoon onto a plate, then top with the chicken slices and garnish with cilantro.

NUTRITION INFORMATION

per serving

calories	fat	sat fat
380	11.7 g	2.5 g

Chicken with mushroom stuffing and butternut squash

prep 30 minutes | **cook** 50 minutes | **serves** 2

for the chicken and stuffing
¼ oz (10 g) dried mushrooms
scant ½ cup boiling water
1 tsp olive oil
scant 1 cup finely chopped fresh brown-cap mushrooms
1 oz (25 g) 95% fat-free soft cheese
2 x 4½ oz (125 g) skinless chicken breasts
freshly ground black pepper, to taste
2 slices prosciutto, trimmed of any fat

for the squash
1 lb 6 oz (625 g), peeled weight, butternut squash, seeded and cut into
    ¾-inch (2-cm) chunks
2 tbsp chopped fresh rosemary
2 tbsp chopped fresh oregano
1 tsp olive oil

1. Preheat the oven to 350°F/180°C.
2. Wash the dried mushrooms, then pour over the boiling water and let stand for 5 minutes. Drain and finely chop.
3. Heat the oil in a nonstick pan, then add the fresh and dried mushrooms and cook over medium heat for 10 minutes, or until they are beginning to brown and any liquid has evaporated. Let cool.
4. Put the soft cheese in a bowl, then stir in the mushrooms and season to taste with pepper. Mix well.
5. Using a sharp knife, make a slit lengthwise in each chicken breast to form a pocket. Spoon in the mushroom mixture. Wrap 1 slice of ham around each breast and enclose in foil to make a package.
6. Put the chunks of squash into a roasting dish. Add the chopped herbs and pepper to taste, then drizzle with the oil. Stir to coat.
7. Place the chicken package on top of the butternut squash and bake for 30 minutes. Remove the foil and return the chicken and squash to the oven for an additional 10 minutes, or until the chicken is cooked. Serve immediately.

COOK'S TIPS
• *You can replace the butternut squash with any other type of squash or pumpkin.*
• *For a different effect, you can purée the cooked squash and serve it topped with the chicken.*

NUTRITION INFORMATION

per serving

calories	fat	sat fat
325	9.5 g	2.4 g

Spanish rice with pork and bell peppers

prep 5 minutes | **cook** 40–50 minutes | **serves** 1

½ tsp olive oil
2¾ oz (75 g) lean pork tenderloin, cut into small cubes
1 small onion, or 2 shallots, peeled and finely chopped
1 garlic clove, peeled and chopped
1 red or orange bell pepper, seeded and chopped into ½-inch (1-cm) squares
7 oz (200 g) canned tomatoes, chopped
1 tbsp chopped fresh parsley
pinch of saffron strands
scant ⅓ cup, dry weight, brown basmati rice
1 cup chicken or vegetable stock
freshly ground black pepper, to taste

1. Heat the oil in a heavy-bottom, lidded, nonstick skillet and brown the pork on all sides on high heat. Remove with a slotted spoon and keep warm.
2. Reduce the heat to medium-high, add the onion, garlic, and bell pepper, and stir-fry for a few minutes until everything is soft and turning golden.
3. Return the meat to the pan, then add the tomatoes, parsley, saffron, rice, and stock and season to taste with pepper. Stir well to combine and to break up the tomatoes a little, and bring to a simmer. Turn the heat down to low and put the lid on.
4. Simmer for 30–40 minutes, or until the rice is tender and all the stock is absorbed. (If the rice is not cooked but the dish looks dry, add a little hot water.)

COOK'S TIPS
• *A good-quality, heavy-bottom pan prevents the rice from sticking or burning as it cooks.*
• *You could use cooked ham instead of pork, but bear in mind that ham is quite salty.*
• *Brown rice adds more fiber and B vitamins, but you can use white rice or easy-cook brown rice if you prefer, following the cooking directions on the package.*

NUTRITION INFORMATION
per serving

calories	fat	sat fat
430	10.2 g	2.6 g

Beef en daube with mustard mash

prep 10 minutes | **cook** 45 minutes–1 hour | **serves** 2

2 tsp vegetable oil
8 oz (225 g) extra-lean braising steak, cut into 8 pieces
10 small shallots, peeled but left whole
1 garlic clove, peeled and crushed
1 medium tomato, chopped
scant 2 cups finely sliced mushrooms
⅔ cup red wine
scant ½ cup chicken stock
1 small bouquet garni
freshly ground black pepper, to taste
1 tsp cornstarch

for the mustard mash
2 medium mealy potatoes, peeled and sliced
¾ fl oz (25 ml) skim milk, heated
1 tsp Dijon mustard, to taste

1. Preheat the oven to 350°F/180°C.
2. Heat the oil in a heavy-bottom flameproof casserole. Add the meat and shallots and cook over high heat, stirring, for 4–5 minutes to brown the meat on all sides. Add the garlic, tomato, mushrooms, wine, and stock and tuck the bouquet garni well in.
3. Bring to a simmer on the stove, then cover and transfer to the oven to cook for 45–60 minutes, or until everything is tender.
4. About 30 minutes before the beef is ready, place the potatoes in boiling water and simmer for 20 minutes, or until just tender. Remove from heat, then drain well and put in a bowl. Add the milk and mash well. Stir in the mustard to taste and keep warm.
5. Use a slotted spoon to remove the meat and vegetables to a warmed serving dish. Cook the sauce on the stove over high heat until reduced by half. Reduce the heat, then remove the bouquet garni and check the seasoning.
6. Add the cornstarch to the sauce, mixed with a little cold water to form a paste, stirring well, and bring back to a simmer. Pour the sauce over the meat and serve with the mustard mash.

COOK'S TIP
• *You could add some ready-cooked black-eye peas, or beans, to the beef if you like. This isn't traditional, but it adds extra fiber and bulk.*

NUTRITION INFORMATION

per serving

calories	fat	sat fat
330	6.4 g	1.6 g

Chili beef with black-eye peas

prep 10 minutes | **cook** 1 hour | **serves** 1

1 tsp olive oil
1 small onion, peeled and finely chopped
1 garlic clove, peeled and crushed or finely chopped
1 small green bell pepper, chopped into ½-inch (1-cm) squares
2¾ oz (75 g) extra-lean braising steak, cut into very small pieces
1 tsp concentrated vegetable stock
2 tsp tomato paste
½ fresh green chili, to taste, seeded and finely chopped
1¾ oz (50 g) canned black-eye peas (or kidney beans), drained and rinsed
3½ oz (100 g) canned tomatoes, chopped
½ tsp chili sauce
freshly ground black pepper, to taste
¼ cup, dry weight, white rice
2 tsp chopped fresh cilantro leaves, to garnish (optional)

1. Heat the oil in a nonstick skillet and sauté the onion, garlic, and bell pepper over medium heat for 2–3 minutes, or until the onion is soft and just turning golden.
2. Add the beef and cook, stirring, until browned on all sides.
3. Add all the remaining ingredients except the rice and cilantro and season to taste with pepper. Stir well and bring to a simmer, then cover and reduce the heat.
4. Cook for 30 minutes, then check the dish for heat, seasoning, and dryness. Add extra chili sauce, very finely chopped fresh chili, or ready-chopped chilies from a jar if it is not hot enough for you, and add water if the sauce looks too dry.
5. Cook for an additional 25–30 minutes, or until the meat is completely tender. Meanwhile, cook the rice according to the directions on the package. Drain and transfer the rice to a warmed plate, then spoon over the sauce and serve garnished with the cilantro, if using.

COOK'S TIPS

• *Chilies vary a great deal in their hotness—it is always best to introduce them cautiously. You can always add more later.*
• *You can make a similar dish using cubed chicken fillet and chicken stock, but the cooking time will need to be reduced to about 30 minutes.*

NUTRITION INFORMATION

per serving

calories	fat	sat fat
445	8.5 g	2.1 g

Nasi goreng

prep 10 minutes | **cook** 20 minutes | **serves** 2

1 cup water
½ cup, dry weight, basmati rice
1 tsp vegetable or olive oil
1 small egg, beaten
1 tsp sesame oil
3½ oz (100 g) turkey fillet, cut into thin, bite-size lengths
1 medium carrot, peeled and cut into thin, bite-size lengths
4 scallions, trimmed and chopped
2 garlic cloves, peeled and crushed
1 fresh hot red chili, seeded and chopped
3½ oz (100 g) cooked, shelled shrimp
scant 1 cup bean sprouts
2 tsp soy sauce
pinch of superfine sugar
chicken stock or water, as necessary

1. Bring the water to a boil in a lidded pan and tip in the rice. Return to a boil, then lower the heat to a simmer. Cover the pan and cook until the rice is tender and all the water absorbed—about 10–15 minutes.
2. Meanwhile, heat the vegetable oil in an individual, nonstick omelet pan (or small skillet). Make the omelet by adding the beaten egg and, when almost set, fold in half, then turn out and slice thinly.
3. When the rice is nearly cooked, heat the sesame oil in a preheated wok or large nonstick skillet and stir-fry the turkey pieces for 1 minute over high heat. Add the carrot, scallions, garlic, and chili and stir-fry for an additional 2 minutes.
4. Reduce the heat, then add the cooked rice to the skillet with the shrimp, bean sprouts, soy sauce, and sugar and stir gently for 1–2 minutes. If the mixture sticks, add a little chicken stock or water.
5. Arrange the omelet slices on top and serve immediately.

NUTRITION INFORMATION

per serving

calories	fat	sat fat
385	7.3 g	1.4 g

Shrimp risotto

prep 10 minutes | **cook** 25 minutes | **serves** 2

1 tsp butter
2 shallots, peeled and finely chopped
1 celery stalk, trimmed and finely chopped
scant ½ cup, dry weight, risotto rice
freshly ground black pepper, to taste
generous ¾ cup hot vegetable or fish stock
scant ½ cup hot water
scant ½ cup white wine
5½ oz (150 g) frozen cooked, shelled shrimp, thawed
4 tsp chopped fresh parsley
1 tbsp light sour cream
dash of lemon juice
1 tsp fresh Parmesan shavings, to serve

1. Heat the butter in a medium-size nonstick skillet over medium heat. When the butter is hot, add the shallots and celery and cook, stirring continuously for 3–4 minutes, or until soft.
2. Add the rice and pepper to taste to the skillet and stir well to coat the rice. Mix the stock and water together. Add just enough of the stock and water mixture to cover the rice and continue to cook, stirring frequently, until it is almost completely absorbed. Continue adding the stock and water in this way until it is almost completely absorbed. Add the wine and continue cooking until that is absorbed.
3. Stir the shrimp and half the parsley into the risotto and heat through.
4. Add the sour cream and lemon juice, then stir and serve immediately with the cheese and the remaining parsley sprinkled over. Accompany with a large mixed side salad with an oil-free French dressing.

COOK'S TIPS
• *If using fresh uncooked shrimp, add them for the last 3 minutes of cooking.*
• *Instead of the shrimp you could use the same quantity of mixed seafood—crabmeat, mussels, squid, etc.*

NUTRITION INFORMATION
per serving

calories	fat	sat fat
340	6.4 g	1.9 g

Mediterranean swordfish sauté with tagliatelle

prep 10 minutes | **cook** 35–40 minutes | **serves** 2

1 tsp olive oil
1 red onion, peeled and finely chopped
1 red bell pepper, seeded and diced
1 garlic clove, peeled and crushed or finely chopped
large pinch of dried chili flakes
1 tsp ground coriander
1 tsp ground cumin
14 oz (400 g) canned tomatoes, chopped
1 tbsp tomato paste
scant ¼ cup red wine
freshly ground black pepper, to taste
9 oz (250 g) swordfish fillet, cubed
2 small zucchini, trimmed and thinly sliced
3½ oz (100 g) dried tagliatelle or pasta shapes, to serve

1. Heat the oil in a large, nonstick, lidded pan. Add the onion, bell pepper, garlic, chili, coriander, and cumin and cook for 5 minutes or until the onions are beginning to soften. Add the tomatoes, tomato paste, and wine and season to taste with pepper. Bring to a boil, then reduce the heat and simmer for about 20 minutes.
2. Add the swordfish and the zucchini to the rest of the ingredients and stir to combine. Bring to simmering point, then cover and cook for 10–12 minutes, or until the sauce is reduced by about half and the zucchini are tender.
3. Meanwhile, cook the tagliatelle according to the package directions, then drain. When the sauce is cooked, pour over the pasta. Serve with a green salad.

COOK'S TIPS
• *Any firm white fish will do instead of swordfish—cod and angler fish are both lower in fat and calories.*
• *You can omit the wine if you wish and add a little fish stock or water instead (fewer calories, but the fish stock is higher in salt).*
• *Canned or bottled sweet bell peppers are quick and easy and give an excellent flavor, but you could use one whole yellow bell pepper instead. Seed and halve, then roast or broil it until tender before slicing.*

NUTRITION INFORMATION

per serving

calories	fat	sat fat
445	8.6 g	1.6 g

Vegetarian entrées

For various reasons, more and more people are choosing not to eat meat or fish. The modern approach to vegetarian cooking and the greater variety and availability of meat-free alternatives means that many more people are choosing to eat at least a couple of meat-free meals during the week. Gone are the days when vegetarian food was considered cranky and boring. Although a vegetarian diet can be a very healthy and balanced way of eating, it often requires a little more thought and planning. The key to a healthy diet—whether you're vegetarian or not—is to eat a variety of foods. The greater the variety of foods you eat, the better chance you'll have of getting the full range of nutrients your body needs. If you cut out meat, it's important to make sure that you eat other foods that provide the vitamins and minerals you would normally get from meat. Meat is an important source of the minerals iron and zinc. If you also cut out dairy products, you'll need to ensure you get enough calcium and vitamin B_{12}.

Vegetable and potato-topped pie

(V) | **prep** 5 minutes | **cook** 50 minutes | **serves** 2

1 lb 2 oz (500 g), peeled weight, potatoes, cut into chunks
2 tbsp lowfat milk
1 tsp olive oil
1 small onion, peeled and finely chopped
scant ¼ cup dried brown lentils (see COOK'S TIPS)
1 garlic clove, peeled and chopped
1 celery stalk, trimmed and finely chopped
scant 1 cup finely chopped brown-cap mushrooms
1 medium carrot, peeled and finely chopped
scant ½ cup vegetable stock
2 tsp vegetarian Worcestershire sauce
14 oz (400 g) canned chopped tomatoes with herbs
1 tsp dried mixed herbs
freshly ground black pepper, to taste
¼ cup grated half-fat Cheddar cheese

1. Preheat the oven to 375°F/190°C.
2. Put the potatoes in a pan with water to cover and bring to a boil, then simmer for 15 minutes, or until tender. Drain and mash the potatoes with the lowfat milk. Set aside.
3. While the potatoes are cooking, heat the oil in a nonstick skillet and sauté the onion over medium heat for a few minutes, stirring occasionally, to soften.
4. Add the lentils, garlic, and celery to the skillet and stir, then add the mushrooms, carrot, stock, Worcestershire sauce, tomatoes, and herbs and stir everything well to combine. Bring to a simmer, then cover and cook gently for 25 minutes, or until you have a rich sauce and the lentils are tender. If the mixture looks too dry during cooking, add a little more stock or water. Taste and season with pepper if necessary.
5. Spoon the lentil mixture into a two-portion baking dish and level the top. Spoon over the mashed potato and sprinkle with the cheese.
6. Bake for 15 minutes, or until the potatoes are golden.

COOK'S TIPS
• The lentil sauce can be also used as a topping for pasta, rice, or baked potatoes. Once made, it can be frozen in single-portion dishes as a handy standby.
• If time is short, replace the dried lentils with 4¼ oz (120 g), drained weight, canned cooked lentils and reduce the cooking time by 15 minutes.

NUTRITION INFORMATION

per serving

calories	fat	sat fat
370	5.2 g	1.7 g

Spinach and mushroom crêpes

(V) | **prep** 15 minutes | **cook** 25–30 minutes | **serves** 2

for the filling
2 tsp vegetable oil
12 oz (350 g) white or brown-cap mushrooms, coarsely chopped
generous ¾ cup vegetable stock
9½ oz (275 g) frozen spinach, thawed and squeezed dry
freshly ground black pepper, to taste
2 tbsp light sour cream

for the crêpes (makes 8)
1 small egg
⅔ cup all-purpose flour
1 tbsp finely chopped fresh parsley
1¼ cups skim milk
lowfat oil spray

1. First, make the filling. Heat the vegetable oil in a nonstick skillet. Add the mushrooms and cook, stirring, for about 5 minutes.
2. Add the stock, spinach, and pepper to taste. Reduce the heat slightly and cook for 10 minutes or until the liquid is thick and syrupy.
3. Meanwhile, make the crêpes. Put the egg, flour, parsley, and milk in an electric blender and blend until smooth.
4. Spray an 8-inch (20-cm) heavy-bottom, nonstick skillet with oil and heat until just smoking. Ladle a little of the batter onto the bottom of the pan and tilt until the whole of the bottom is thinly coated. Cook the crêpe for 1 minute and then flip over and cook the other side for 1 minute.
5. Put the crêpe on a plate over a pan of gently simmering water to keep warm, and continue making crêpes until all the batter is used up.
6. When the mushrooms are ready, stir in the sour cream. Spoon one-eighth of the filling into the center of each crêpe. Fold each crêpe in half and serve with steamed vegetables, such as broccoli.

COOK'S TIP
• *You can freeze any excess crêpes in single portions, then reheat them in a nonstick skillet. Just be sure to put wax paper between the crêpes prior to freezing.*

NUTRITION INFORMATION
per serving (i.e. 4 crêpes)

calories	fat	sat fat
324	10.4 g	1.6 g

Moroccan vegetable tagine

Ⓥ | **prep** 5 minutes | **cook** 45 minutes | **serves** 2

1 tsp olive oil
1 medium onion, peeled and chopped
1 garlic clove, peeled and chopped
½ tsp ground anise
2 green cardamom pods, "bruised" by lightly rolling with a rolling pin
½ fresh red chili, seeded and finely chopped
1¼ cups hot vegetable stock
7 oz (200 g) canned tomatoes, chopped
1¾ oz (50 g), peeled weight, turnip or parsnip, or rutabaga or pumpkin, diced
1 medium potato, peeled and diced
1 small carrot, peeled and diced
2¾ oz (75 g), drained weight, canned chickpeas, rinsed
½ cinnamon stick
1 small zucchini, trimmed and diced
scant ¼ cup dried dates, chopped
generous ⅓ cup no-soak dried apricots, chopped

for the couscous
1¾ oz (50 g), dry weight, couscous
scant ½ cup hot vegetable stock

1. Heat the oil in a large, lidded, nonstick pan over medium heat. Add the onion and garlic and sauté for about 5 minutes, or until soft. Reduce the heat, then add the spices and cook for 1 minute, stirring.
2. Add the hot stock, tomatoes, turnip, potato, carrot, chickpeas, and cinnamon and bring to a boil. Reduce the heat, then cover and simmer for 30 minutes, stirring occasionally.
3. Add the zucchini, dates, and apricots to the pan, plus a little water if needed. Replace the lid and cook for an additional 15 minutes, or until the fruit has absorbed the liquid.
4. Meanwhile, prepare the couscous according to the directions on the package using the hot stock. Fork through to separate the grains, then transfer to a warmed dish and serve with the sauce.

COOK'S TIP
• *This sauce becomes even tastier if stored refrigerated for 1–2 days before eating.*

NUTRITION INFORMATION
per serving

calories	fat	sat fat
340	4.2 g	0.5 g

Fall vegetable gratin

Ⓥ | **prep** 10 minutes | **cook** 30–35 minutes | **serves** 1

7 oz (200 g) canned chopped tomatoes
scant 1 cup sliced closed-cap mushrooms
scant ½ cup, shelled weight, fava beans, fresh or frozen
3½ oz (100 g), peeled weight, butternut squash, cut into ½-inch (1-cm) slices,
    then cut into fourths
1 medium zucchini, trimmed and cut into ¼-inch (½-cm) slices
2 scallions, trimmed and finely chopped
freshly ground black pepper, to taste
few fresh basil leaves (optional)
½ oz (15 g) reduced-fat hard cheese, such as sharp Cheddar, or a vegetarian
    Parmesan or romano
1 tbsp fresh bread crumbs

1. Put the tomatoes, mushrooms, beans, and squash into a pan and bring to a simmer, then cover and simmer over low heat for 15 minutes. Add the zucchini and scallions and cook for an additional 5–10 minutes, or until tender, adding a very little water if the chopped tomatoes don't cover all the vegetables.
2. Season to taste with pepper and stir in the basil, if using, then tip the mixture into an individual gratin dish and smooth out.
3. Preheat the broiler to medium-high. Mix together the cheese and bread crumbs and sprinkle over the top. Brown under the broiler for 1–2 minutes, or until golden. Serve immediately.

COOK'S TIP
• *Fresh or frozen corn can be used instead of fava beans.*

NUTRITION INFORMATION
per serving

calories	fat	sat fat
180	3.9 g	1.6 g

Mediterranean vegetables
with goat cheese and penne

(V) | **prep** 5 minutes | **cook** 15–20 minutes | **serves** 1

scant ½ cup dried penne pasta
1 small red bell pepper, seeded and cut into bite-size chunks
1 small zucchini, trimmed and cut into bite-size slices
1 small red onion, peeled and cut into wedges
1 tsp olive oil
freshly ground black pepper, to taste
12 cherry tomatoes, halved
3 pitted black olives, halved
1¼ oz (35 g) goat cheese, crumbled
few fresh basil leaves, to garnish

for the dressing
2 tsp balsamic vinegar
1 tsp lemon juice
1 tsp torn fresh basil leaves

1. Put a pan of water on to boil and preheat the broiler to medium-high. Cook the pasta according to the package directions.
2. Arrange the bell pepper, zucchini, and onion on a nonstick baking sheet, then brush with the oil and season to taste with pepper. Broil for about 5 minutes. Turn the pieces and continue broiling for an additional 5 minutes, or until tender.
3. When the pasta is cooked, drain well and transfer to a serving bowl. Stir in the cherry tomatoes, olives, and the charbroiled vegetables with their oil and juices.
4. Beat together the dressing ingredients and stir into the pasta. Crumble over the goat cheese, then garnish with basil and serve.

COOK'S TIPS
• *For a change, try adding a couple of drained canned artichoke hearts or cooked fresh asparagus to the vegetables.*
• *Ideal served with a mixed green salad.*

NUTRITION INFORMATION

per serving

calories	fat	sat fat
370	11.6 g	4.3 g

Quick mushroom risotto

V | **prep** 5 minutes + 30 minutes soaking | **cook** 30 minutes | **serves** 1

1 tbsp dried porcini mushrooms
1 tsp olive oil
1 tsp butter
½ medium onion, peeled and finely chopped
1 small garlic clove, peeled and finely chopped
5½ oz (150 g) mixed fresh mushrooms (e.g. cremini, shiitake, white)
freshly ground black pepper, to taste
generous ¼ cup, dry weight, risotto rice
generous ¾ cup vegetable stock
scant ¼ cup dry white wine (or extra stock)
1 small zucchini, trimmed and chopped
1 tsp chopped fresh parsley
1 tsp freshly grated vegetarian Parmesan or romano cheese

1. Put the dried mushrooms in a bowl, then cover with water and let soak for 30 minutes (see COOK'S TIPS).
2. About 5 minutes before the soaking time is up, heat the oil and butter in a large, lidded, nonstick skillet and sauté the onion and garlic over medium heat for 5 minutes, or until soft. Add the fresh mushrooms and pepper to taste, then stir well and cook for 1–2 minutes.
3. Add the rice and soaked mushrooms with their soaking water, stock, and wine, if using, and stir. Cover and simmer for 20 minutes, adding a little extra stock or water if it looks dry. Add the zucchini and continue to simmer for an additional 10 minutes.
4. When the rice is tender and creamy, stir in the parsley and Parmesan cheese. Serve the risotto with a mixed salad.

COOK'S TIPS
• *Don't use flat portobello mushrooms as their juices will make the dish go black.*
• *This is an alternative and quick method to cook risotto.*

NUTRITION INFORMATION

per serving

calories	fat	sat fat
435	11.4 g	4.5 g

Vegetable korma with cardamom-scented rice

(V) | prep 10 minutes | cook 35–40 minutes | serves 1

for the vegetable korma
1 tsp vegetable oil
1 small onion, peeled and thinly sliced
1 small garlic clove, peeled and crushed
¼ tsp ground cumin
¼ tsp ground coriander
¼ tsp turmeric
¼ tsp garam masala
generous pinch of ground ginger
1 small potato, peeled and cut into bite-size pieces, then parboiled
   for 5 minutes
½ small eggplant, cut into ½-inch (1-cm) slices and then into fourths
1 oz (25 g) green beans, trimmed and halved
¾ cup vegetable stock
1 tsp ground almonds
scant ½ cup strained plain yogurt

for the cardamom-scented rice
¼ cup basmati rice
2 green cardamom pods, lightly crushed
⅔ cup water

1. First, prepare the korma. Heat the oil in a nonstick skillet and stir-fry the onion on medium-high until soft (about 3–4 minutes). Add the garlic and spices and stir for 1 minute.
2. Add the potato, eggplant, beans, and half the stock, then stir well and bring to a simmer. Reduce the heat and simmer gently for 20 minutes, adding more stock if the mixture looks too dry.
3. Meanwhile, rinse the rice in cold water and put in a small, lidded pan, along with the cardamom pods. Cover with the water and bring to a boil, then reduce the heat and cook, covered, for 15 minutes, or until tender.
4. Add the ground almonds for the last 2 minutes of cooking the korma.
5. When the vegetables are cooked, add the yogurt and stir well. Heat for 1–2 minutes (but don't boil). Remove the cardamom pods from the rice and serve the korma on a bed of the cooked rice.

NUTRITION INFORMATION

per serving

calories	fat	sat fat
430	9 g	1.6 g

Sweet potato curry with lentils

Ⓥ | **prep** 5–7 minutes | **cook** 40 minutes | **serves** 1

1 tsp vegetable oil
3½ oz (100 g), peeled weight, sweet potato, cut into bite-size cubes
2¾ oz (75 g), peeled weight, potato, cut into bite-size cubes
1 small onion, peeled and finely chopped
1 small garlic clove, peeled and finely chopped
1 small fresh green chili, seeded and chopped
½ tsp ground ginger
¼ cup dried green lentils
generous ¼ cup–scant ½ cup hot vegetable stock
freshly ground black pepper, to taste
½ tsp garam masala
generous ¼ cup–scant ½ cup hot water
1 tbsp lowfat plain yogurt

1. Heat the oil in a nonstick, lidded pan and sauté the sweet potato over medium heat, turning occasionally, for 5 minutes.
2. Meanwhile, bring the potato to a boil in a pan of water, then simmer until almost cooked (about 6 minutes). Drain and set aside.
3. When the sweet potato cubes are sautéed, remove them with a slotted spoon and add in the onion. Cook, stirring occasionally, for 5 minutes, or until transparent. Add the garlic, chili, and ginger and stir for 1 minute.
4. Return the sweet potato to the pan with the boiled potato and the lentils, half the stock, pepper to taste, and garam masala. Stir to combine, bring to a simmer, and cover. Reduce the heat and simmer gently for 20 minutes, adding a little more stock if the the curry looks too dry.
5. Stir in the yogurt and serve with boiled basmati rice.

COOK'S TIPS
• *Scratch the skin of the sweet potato to make sure it is orange-fleshed—the white-fleshed variety is not so good in this recipe.*
• *You could replace sweet potato with pumpkin or butternut squash.*

NUTRITION INFORMATION

per serving

calories	fat	sat fat
315	4.9 g	0.9 g

Tofu and vegetable stir-fry with rice noodles

(V) | **prep** 15 minutes + 2 hours marinating | **cook** 10 minutes | **serves** 1

100 g (3½ oz) firm tofu, sliced into strips (see COOK'S TIP)

for the marinade
1 tsp soy sauce
1 tbsp lime juice
1 tsp chopped garlic
1 tsp chopped lemongrass
1 tsp chopped fresh gingerroot
1 tsp chopped fresh red chili

1¾ oz (50 g) dried rice noodles
1 tsp vegetable oil
1¾ oz (50 g) bok choy, coarsely chopped
1¾ oz (50 g) broccoli florets, coarsely chopped
1 small carrot, peeled and cut into thin strips
⅓ cup bean sprouts
1 tsp vegetarian Thai green curry paste
2 tbsp vegetable stock
2 scallions, trimmed and halved lengthwise

1. Put the tofu in a shallow dish. Whisk together the soy sauce and lime juice and pour over the tofu with the other marinade ingredients. If possible, let marinate for at least 2 hours (see COOK'S TIP).
2. Cook the noodles according to the package directions. Drain and keep warm.
3. Heat the oil in a nonstick wok or large skillet. Remove the tofu from the marinade, reserving the marinade, and stir-fry the tofu for 1 minute. Add the bok choy, broccoli, carrots, and bean sprouts and cook, stirring, for an additional 1 minute.
4. In a small bowl or cup, mix the curry paste, stock, and reserved marinade together. Add half to the stir-fry mixture and cook for an additional 2 minutes.
5. Add the remaining paste and marinade mix and the scallions to the stir-fry and cook for 1 minute, or until the vegetables are just tender. Serve on a bed of warm noodles.

COOK'S TIPS
• *Drain the tofu and wash under a running faucet, then remove excess water with paper towels.*
• *Make time to marinate the tofu, as it is quite bland but takes up other flavors well.*

NUTRITION INFORMATION
per serving
(not including the vegetarian Thai green curry paste)

calories	fat	sat fat
360	9.4 g	1.3 g

Vegetables
and side dishes

Vegetable accompaniments and side dishes provide the perfect opportunity to boost both the amount and variety of vegetables in your diet. Although many people automatically assume that fresh is best, frozen and canned vegetables also have much to offer. Frozen vegetables are processed within hours of being harvested, so their vitamin content is preserved. Studies show that in some cases frozen vegetables actually contain more vitamins than "fresh" vegetables, which may well be a few days old by the time we use them. The vitamins in vegetables are easily lost during storage, preparation, and cooking—to maximize your vitamin content, the golden rule is to buy the freshest produce available, then store in the refrigerator and eat as soon as possible after purchase. Once cut, the vitamin C will react with the oxygen in the air and be lost, so it's important not to prepare vegetables too far in advance of cooking and eating.

Potatoes à la boulangère

V | **prep** 15 minutes | **cook** 1 hour | **serves** 2

14 oz (400 g), peeled weight, potatoes, very thinly sliced
1 small onion, peeled and thinly sliced
freshly ground black pepper, to taste
generous ¼ cup vegetable stock (see COOK'S TIP)
generous ¼ cup skim milk
1 tsp butter

1. Preheat the oven to 350°F/180°C.
2. Layer the potato and onion slices in a shallow, ovenproof dish, seasoning each layer well with pepper.
3. Mix the stock and milk together and pour over the potatoes. Dot the top layer with the butter, then cover with foil and bake in the oven for 30 minutes.
4. Remove the foil and continue to cook for an additional 30 minutes, or until the potatoes are cooked.

COOK'S TIPS
• *You can use an alternative to the onion such as leeks or mixed bell peppers.*
• *You could use chicken stock instead of vegetable stock if catering for non-vegetarians.*

NUTRITION INFORMATION

per serving

calories	fat	sat fat
200	2.8 g	1.5 g

Spinach and butternut squash bake

(V) | **prep** 20 minutes | **cook** 40 minutes | **serves** 2

for the baked vegetables
9 oz (250 g), peeled weight, butternut squash, seeded and cut into
   bite-size cubes
2 small red onions, peeled and each cut into 8 segments
2 tsp light vegetable or olive oil
freshly ground black pepper, to taste
4¼ oz (120 g) baby spinach leaves
1 tbsp water

for the white sauce
1 cup skim milk
scant ¼ cup cornstarch
1 tsp mustard powder
1 small onion, peeled
2 small bay leaves
4 tsp freshly grated vegetarian Parmesan or Pecorino cheese

for the topping
2 tbsp fresh whole-wheat bread crumbs

1. Preheat the oven to 400°F/200°C and warm an ovenproof serving dish.
2. Arrange the prepared squash and onions on a nonstick baking sheet and coat with the oil
and plenty of pepper. Bake for 20 minutes, turning once.
3. To make the sauce, put the milk into a small nonstick pan with the cornstarch, mustard, onion,
and bay leaves. Whisk over medium heat until thick. Remove from the heat, then discard the
onion and bay leaves and stir in the cheese. Set aside, stirring occasionally, to prevent a skin
forming.
4. When the squash is nearly cooked, put the spinach in a large pan with the water, stirring, for
2–3 minutes, or until just wilted.
5. You can continue cooking this dish in the hot oven, or preheat the broiler to medium-high.
Put half the squash mixture in the warmed ovenproof dish and top with half the spinach.
Repeat the layers. Pour over the white sauce and sprinkle over the bread crumbs.
6. Either put under the preheated broiler until browned and bubbling, or transfer to the oven
for 15–20 minutes.

COOK'S TIP
• *Lightly boiled, steamed, or microwaved cauliflower florets can be added to the squash for extra bulk.*

NUTRITION INFORMATION

per serving

calories	fat	sat fat
120	3.9 g	1.4 g

Sweet and sour red cabbage

Ⓥ | **prep** 5 minutes | **cook** 45–55 minutes | **serves** 2

7 oz (200 g) red cabbage, prepared weight, any tough core removed,
 finely sliced
1 medium cooking apple, peeled, cored, and chopped
1 shallot, peeled and finely chopped
1 tbsp wine vinegar, red or white
1 tbsp brown sugar
1 tsp butter
2 tbsp water
freshly ground black pepper, to taste

1. Put all the ingredients in a heavy-bottom, lidded pan or flameproof casserole.
Season to taste with pepper.
2. Cook over medium-low heat for 15 minutes, then stir well and replace the lid.
Reduce the heat and simmer for 30–40 minutes, stirring once or twice.
3. When the cabbage is tender, check the seasoning and serve.

COOK'S TIP
• *This dish can also be cooked in the oven, 325°F/160°C, for the
 same amount of time.*

NUTRITION INFORMATION

per serving

calories	fat	sat fat
105	2.5 g	1.4 g

Zucchini with mustard seeds

Ⓥ | **prep** 5 minutes | **cook** 10–15 minutes | **serves** 2

1 tsp vegetable or
  olive oil
1 garlic clove, peeled and crushed
½ tsp black mustard seeds
½ tsp ground cumin
½ tsp coriander seeds
½ fresh red chili, seeded and
  finely chopped
2 medium zucchini, trimmed
  and sliced
7 oz (200 g) canned tomatoes,
  chopped
1 tbsp chopped fresh cilantro leaves
  or parsley

1. Heat the oil in a nonstick, lidded pan. Add the garlic, dry spices, and chili and stir over medium heat, then remove from the heat for 2 minutes.
2. Add the zucchini and tomatoes and cook for about 5–10 minutes, or until tender, adding 1 tablespoon of water if necessary. Stir in the cilantro and serve.

COOK'S TIP
- *As a change from zucchini, try okra or serve the sauce over green beans.*

Glazed parsnips with sesame seeds

Ⓥ | **prep** 5 minutes | **cook** 20 minutes | **serves** 2

2 parsnips, peeled and cut into
  even-size chunks
1 tsp runny honey
½ tsp sesame seeds

Opposite fore-ground: Glazed parsnips with sesame seeds; background: Zucchini with mustard seeds

1. Preheat the oven to 400°F/200°C.
2. Put the parsnips in a pan of water, bring to a boil, and cook for 5 minutes. Drain well.
3. Transfer the parsnips to a roasting pan and brush with the honey, then roast in the oven for 10 minutes.
4. Sprinkle over the sesame seeds and cook for an additional 5 minutes.

COOK'S TIP
- *You can prepare carrots in the same way.*

NUTRITION INFORMATION

per serving

calories	fat	sat fat
60	2.5 g	0.5 g

NUTRITION INFORMATION

per serving

calories	fat	sat fat
100	2.0 g	0.4 g

Desserts

You don't have to miss out on dessert just because you're on a diet. Desserts don't have to be high in fat and sugar. Fresh fruit or a fruit salad is an excellent way to finish a meal and will help you reach the recommended target of 5 daily servings of fruit and/or vegetables. But if you fancy something a little more decadent, there are plenty of lowfat options available. Presentation plays an important role in our enjoyment of food and can transform a simple dessert into a special one. A sprig of fresh mint, a light dusting of confectioners' sugar, or a slice of fresh fruit as a garnish can make a real difference.

Meringues with lime cream and raspberries

(V) | **prep** 5 minutes | **serves** 1

2½ tbsp plain yogurt (less than 2% fat)
2 tsp confectioners' sugar
grated zest and juice of ¼ lime
1 meringue nest
scant ¼ cup raspberries

1. Mix the yogurt, confectioners' sugar, and lime zest and juice together.
2. Place a meringue nest on a plate and pour in the yogurt mixture, then sprinkle with raspberries and serve.

COOK'S TIP
• *You can substitute frozen fruits of the forest for the raspberries or use fresh fruit in season.*

NUTRITION INFORMATION

per serving

calories	fat	sat fat
135	0.5 g	0.3 g

Strawberry and orange delight

prep 10 minutes + 30 minutes cooling | **cook** 5 minutes | **serves** 2

1¾ cups orange juice (see COOK'S TIP)
1 tbsp gelatin, or vegetarian equivalent (gelozone)
3¼ oz (90 g) small strawberries, sliced

1. Put scant ½ cup of the juice in a small heatproof bowl, then sprinkle over the gelatin and let stand for 5 minutes. Place the bowl over a pan of simmering water and stir until the gelatin melts and the liquid becomes clear, then stir in the remaining juice.
2. Divide the strawberries between 2 large wine glasses. Pour over enough juice to just cover the strawberries, then transfer to the refrigerator for 30 minutes, or until set.
3. Pour in the remaining juice and return to the refrigerator until set.

COOK'S TIPS
• When strawberries are out of season, use seedless grapes instead.
• You could use another juice instead of orange, such as passion fruit (but not pineapple).

NUTRITION INFORMATION
per serving

calories	fat	sat fat
130	0.2 g	trace

Spiced pineapple with mango sauce

(V) | **prep** 10 minutes | **cook** 5 minutes | **serves** 2

for the sauce
1 small ripe mango, peeled and pitted
½ cup orange juice
1 tsp arrowroot
½ tsp allspice
1 tsp melted butter
2 tsp raw sugar

2 thick slices fresh pineapple

1. First, make the sauce. Put the mango and orange juice in an electric blender and purée until smooth. Tip the purée into a small pan. Mix the arrowroot with a little cold water and add to the pan. Heat gently, stirring constantly, until the sauce begins to thicken.
2. Preheat the broiler to medium-high. Stir the allspice into the melted butter. Place the pineapple on a foil-covered baking sheet. Brush the pineapple with the melted butter, then sprinkle over the sugar and put under the broiler for 5 minutes.
3. Transfer the pineapple to a plate, then pour over a little of the sauce and serve warm (see COOK'S TIP).

COOK'S TIP
• *Decorate with delicate cape gooseberries for that added touch.*

NUTRITION INFORMATION

per serving

calories	fat	sat fat
145	2.4 g	1.4 g

Roasted peach with vanilla sugar

Ⓥ | **prep** 10 minutes | **cook** 15–20 minutes | **serves** 1

for the vanilla sugar
¼ vanilla bean
scant 2 tbsp superfine sugar

1 small ripe peach, halved and pitted
2 tbsp lowfat plain yogurt

1. Preheat the oven to 400°F/200°C.
2. Scrape out the sticky seeds from the vanilla bean and blend with the sugar in an electric hand blender.
3. Place the peach, flesh-side up, in an ovenproof dish and sprinkle over the vanilla sugar.
4. Bake for 15–20 minutes, or until tender, and serve with plain yogurt.

COOK'S TIPS
• *If your peach is under-ripe, allow 20–30 minutes cooking time.*
• *This dish also works well with nectarines and plums—allow 1 nectarine or 2 plums per serving.*
• *A batch of vanilla sugar can be made ahead and kept for several weeks in a jar.*

NUTRITION INFORMATION
per serving

calories	fat	sat fat
140	0.2 g	0.2 g

Apple phyllo pockets with vanilla yogurt

Ⓥ | **prep** 5 minutes | **cook** 20–25 minutes | **serves** 2

for phyllo pockets (makes 2)
1 medium tart cooking apple, peeled, cored, and cut into small chunks
2 tsp water
½ oz (15 g) golden raisins
2 tsp sugar
1 tsp lemon juice
pinch of ground cinnamon
6 sheets phyllo pastry, approximately ¾ x 1¼ inches (2 x 3 cm)
1 egg white, beaten
1 tbsp skim milk

for vanilla yogurt
few drops of vanilla extract
scant ½ cup lowfat plain yogurt, to serve

1. Preheat the oven to 400°F/200°C.
2. Put the apples in a small pan with the water. Simmer over gentle heat for a few minutes, or until the apples are just soft. Take care not to overcook the apples, as they will continue cooking in the oven.
3. Drain any excess liquid from the apples, then stir in the golden raisins, sugar, lemon juice, and cinnamon.
4. Take 3 sheets of phyllo, one on top of the other, and brush with the egg white. Spoon the apple mixture into the center and gather up the pastry edges to form a bag around the filling. Pinch the phyllo together with your fingers to seal it. Repeat with the remaining 3 sheets. Work quickly with the phyllo, as it goes dry quickly.
5. Place the pockets on a baking sheet and brush with the milk.
6. Bake for 20–25 minutes, or until golden brown. Let cool for a few minutes.
7. Stir the vanilla extract into the yogurt and serve with the phyllo pockets.

NUTRITION INFORMATION

per serving

calories	fat	sat fat
150	1.1 g	0.3 g

Baked banana with sin-free chocolate sauce

Ⓥ | **prep** 1 minute | **cook** 10 minutes | **serves** 1

1 small banana
2 tsp corn syrup
3 tsp unsweetened cocoa

1. Preheat the oven to 350°F/180°C.
2. Bake the banana in its skin for 10 minutes, or until the skin is black.
3. Meanwhile, warm the syrup in a small pan over medium heat for 2–3 minutes, or in a medium-low microwave for 1 minute until very runny. Stir in the unsweetened cocoa until smooth and chocolate-like. Keep warm.
4. When the banana is cooked, discard the skin and put the flesh on a plate, then pour the chocolate sauce over and serve.

COOK'S TIP
• *You could, alternatively, bake your bananas on the grill until their skins turn black.*

NUTRITION INFORMATION

per serving

calories	fat	sat fat
140	2.6 g	0.6 g

Chocolate and orange liqueur mousse

prep 5 minutes + 40 minutes soaking | serves 1

Opposite left:
Chocolate and
orange liqueur
mousse; right:
Rum and raisin
chocolate mousse

½ tsp grated orange zest
1 tsp Cointreau
2½ oz (70 g) lowfat chocolate mousse
1 meringue nest, lightly crushed

1. Put the zest in an eggcup with the Cointreau and soak for at least 30 minutes.
2. Put the chocolate mousse in a bowl and stir in the meringue. Spoon into a sundae dish (see COOK'S TIP).
3. Refrigerate for at least 10 minutes, then serve with the orange zest and Cointreau spooned over.

COOK'S TIP

• *For an attractive layered effect (as shown opposite), spoon half the chocolate mousse into a sundae dish, followed by the meringue, followed by the rest of the mousse.*

Rum and raisin chocolate mousse

prep 10 minutes + 30 minutes soaking | serves 1

1 tsp raisins
1 tbsp dark rum
1 amaretto cookie, crumbled (optional)
2½ oz (70 g) lowfat chocolate mousse

1. Put the raisins in a teacup, then pour over the rum and let stand for at least 30 minutes, preferably overnight.
2. Stir the rum, raisins, and amaretto cookie into the chocolate mousse. Spoon into a sundae dish and serve.

COOK'S TIP

• *Amaretti cookies are a useful ingredient for slimming desserts because they are very light and are only 8% fat, but use them sparingly, as they are high in sugar.*

NUTRITION INFORMATION

per serving

calories	fat	sat fat
140	1.9 g	trace

NUTRITION INFORMATION

per serving

calories	fat	sat fat
150	2.3 g	1.2 g

Pear and chocolate cream

prep 5 minutes │ can be made ahead and chilled │ **serves** 1

2¾ oz (75 g), drained weight, canned pears in juice
generous ⅓ cup virtually fat-free ricotta
few drops of vanilla extract
½ square milk chocolate, grated

1. Purée the pears in an electric blender, or mash thoroughly with a fork.
2. In a mixing bowl, combine the pears, ricotta, and vanilla extract, then lightly stir in two-thirds of the chocolate.
3. Spoon into a single-serving dessert glass or dish and top with the remaining chocolate. Chill before serving.

NUTRITION INFORMATION

per serving

calories	fat	sat fat
150	4.7 g	2.7 g

Index